Cathy:

May the Lord
God Almighty lead
you to learn and
His will. Blessed be
name!

Blessings, Debbie
5/10

MW01378725

THE REDEEMED OF THE LORD

A Call to Pray

Written By Debbie Haskell

AuthorHouse™
1663 Liberty Drive, Suite 200
Bloomington, IN 47403
www.authorhouse.com
Phone: 1-800-839-8640

© 2009 Debbie Haskell. All rights reserved.

No part of this book may be reproduced, stored in a retrieval system, or transmitted by any means without the written permission of the author.

First published by AuthorHouse   2/11/2009

ISBN: 978-1-4389-1340-7 (sc)

Printed in the United States of America
Bloomington, Indiana

This book is printed on acid-free paper.

*This book is dedicated to my mother,
Pearl Haskell, whom the Lord
called home during its writing.*

*Mom, your sweet, precious spirit is
missed by us all. We love you!*

Contents

Acknowledgments...........................ix

Opening Thoughts

A Call to Pray............................... 1
A God Who Loves 7

Lessons I Have Learned

The Father of the Fatal 17
Eyes Wide Open............................ 25
Heart Wide Open.......................... 33
Praying on the Edge 45

Closing Remarks

Answering the Call to Pray................. 55
Give Praise 63

Endnotes.................................. 69
Sources 71

Acknowledgments

Many projects like this, whether big or small, begin with the encouragement of a friend or loved one. This book has been no exception. Before I ever put pen to paper or even knew the subject of this book, my sweet friend, Judy Dunham, encouraged me to speak my heart through the words I would write. Thank you, Judy, for your encouragement and faith in me.

Candace Cain was my patient listener and reader. I lost count of the number of times I went to her office to bounce off an idea or show her the next chapter. Thanks, Candace!

I am grateful to Julie Piazza, who read the manuscript and offered several wonderful suggestions. Thanks, Julie. You are a God-send!

Thank you to John and Mary Barton and Patrick Mead, who proofread this text.

A special thanks to Chris Lindsey for pictures, graphics, and cover design, and to Jodie Anspach for her help with pictures, and to Phil Conner for his computer assistance.

Lastly, I am deeply grateful to Zack DePew and Lynn Ingogly, my editors, whose fine editing skills brought my thoughts and ideas to the next level.

Opening Thoughts

✣ ✣ ✣

A Call to Pray

❖ ❖ ❖

*May we, oh Lord God,
who are Your children, Your people, Your redeemed,
hear the call on our hearts to pray for those
who do not yet know You
as their Heavenly Father.*

❖ ❖ ❖

Forever engraved on our minds, whether Americans or not, are the images of September 11, 2001.

Like many of you, I will always remember where I was when I first heard the news of that horrific day. At the time, I was teaching English at a small Christian college. I was in my office preparing for a class later that morning when Ronnie, one of the information technology (IT) guys, came flying out of his office yelling, "People, come quick! You're not going to believe what just happened!"

Several people came running, myself included, and Ronnie told us that a plane had just flown into one of the World Trade Center buildings in New York City. I looked at him rather dazed, my mind not really comprehending what he had said. Ronnie hooked up a line to the monitor in the IT room, and a handful of us stood there watching as one of the towers was engulfed in flames.

Then, to our utter disbelief, we saw another plane fly into the other tower.

Along with all of you, I stood there watching an event with my eyes that neither my mind nor my heart could begin to grasp. I was stunned.

As the day progressed, classes at the college were canceled, and our small community gathered in our assembly hall to watch the day's events on the big screen. I doubt any of us will forget that day.

Later that afternoon, the weekly prayer group that I was involved with at the time gathered to pray. We were a small group, four women, but we wanted to pray for the victims, the survivors, our leaders, and God's presence.

During the weeks that followed, we continued to pray about that day—a day that had forever changed the America we knew. We prayed for all the people affected, for protection for this country, and for the capture of those responsible for such despicable acts. After several weeks,

I discovered a growing desire in my heart to pray for the Muslim nations. Of course, I prayed against any militant movements that would continue to terrorize this country, or any other, but I also began to pray for the Muslim people. I realized that the militant group of Muslims who committed such terrible acts was not the everyday Muslims who were walking the streets of America—or even the Middle East—and my heart grieved for the way these people were sometimes treated. Eventually, I began to pray that these people would come to know the God of heaven and His Son, Jesus Christ, as their Savior.

More than six years later, that prayer still continues. I wrote this book to ask you to please join me in this prayer. And lest you think that I am only asking for prayers for people of the Islamic faith, please, allow me to continue with my story.

In the months and years that followed 9/11, I felt a burden on my heart to pray for another group of people, and just this past fall, I added a third group to my prayer list. My desire in writing this book is not only to call us to pray over a host of issues, but also to share what I have discovered about praying for the lost. We, as the redeemed of the Lord, play a crucial role in the salvation of our world. Only Jesus, of course, saves people from their sins, but He did leave the spreading of that message in our hands. Not all of us can be missionaries. Not all of us can teach Bible classes. Not all of us can be speakers or writers. But all of us can pray!

The purpose of this book is to call the redeemed of the Lord to pray for a lost world. Specifically, I am asking each individual Christian to open his or her heart to a commitment to pray for an individual, a group of people, or a specific issue. I will address this request in greater detail in the closing section of this book.

But first, I would like to offer some thoughts about the God who loves us so much He chose to become human and die for us on a Roman cross, and secondly, to share some of the lessons that I have learned as I have prayed for the lost over the past few years.

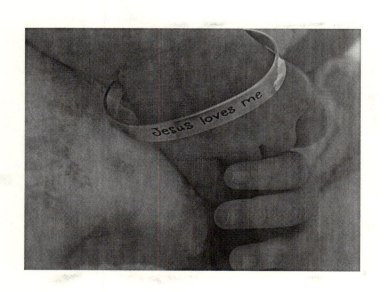

A God Who Loves

✤ ✤ ✤

*May You, oh Giver of all that is good,
shower us with Your divine love.
May this sacrificial and unconditional love
transform us into the likeness of Your Son.*

God loves people. As a matter of fact, people are the most precious creatures on earth to God. I sometimes ask myself why God loves us so. After all, we can be pretty unlovable at times. For instance, I sometimes picture unbelievers as a group of people who live in the goodness and care of a Heavenly Father yet refuse to recognize or acknowledge the One who makes their very lives possible. And I picture believers as a group of people who sometimes are reluctant to be transformed by God's presence and the power of His word.

Describing all the possible individual circumstances that may exist in the two sweeping statements above is not the intent of this book. Suffice it to say that all of us, believers or not, have hurt the heart of a loving God. This does not change the fact, though, that God loves all of us.

As the redeemed of the Lord, we believers are privileged to know the Father who abides in heaven, His Son who died for us, and the Holy Spirit who lives in us. Though the concept of the Trinity may be beyond our understanding, what is not is the love this Triune God has shown to His creation. Words do not exist on this side of eternity to fully express the depth of love the Father in heaven has for His children. The Bible captures the idea, however, in John 3:16, "For God so loved the world that he gave his one and only Son, that whoever believes in him shall not perish but have eternal life." [1]

The love of the Father is the most precious gift the Almighty can bestow on us, for His love is complete, embracing eternal wisdom, peace, grace, joy, and all the other divine attributes that make our God who He is. God's love for humankind is so profound that He willingly shares His perfect love with an imperfect world. We know that mature love is sacrificial; it seeks the best interests of the beloved. We see this love in action by God the Father in the sacrifice of Jesus, His Son. What better way could God show us the depth of His love than by dying on the cross to redeem our souls for eternal life with Him? God loves us—all of us. And He sacrificed His Son to show us that is so!

And how does one describe Jesus's willingness to leave heaven and live and die on this earth? The Bible expresses the idea in Philippians 2:5–8:

> Your attitude should be the same as that of Christ Jesus: Who, being in very nature God, did not consider equality with God something to be grasped, but made Himself nothing, taking the very nature of a servant, being made in human likeness. And being found in appearance as a man, He humbled Himself and became obedient to death—even death on a cross! [2]

The sacrifice of Jesus is truly unfathomable. I have no idea what heaven will be like, but I feel confident saying that once I am there, residing in the presence of perfect love, I will not want to leave. I can only imagine the distress suffered by the Godhead as Jesus willingly left heaven to take up residence on the earth. The life and death of the Savior express a depth of love which gives the word "love" tangibility. Jesus shows us divine love in action—action that shows us and teaches us the way divine love acts, responds, and gives. In the life of Jesus, we see the definition of love. I doubt, however, that I can fully grasp the definition or the sacrifice on this side of eternity.

How do we even begin to comprehend the role the Holy Spirit plays in our lives? For He lives within us and guarantees our inheritance with the God of all the universe. As 1 Corinthians 6:19–20 states, "Do you not know that your body is a temple of the Holy Spirit, who is in you, whom you have received from God? You are not your own; you were bought at a price. Therefore honor God with your body." [3] Ephesians 1:13–14 also tells us, "Having believed, you were marked in Him with a seal, the promised Holy Spirit, who is a deposit guaranteeing our inheritance until the redemption of those who are God's possession—to the praise of His glory." [4] The unsearchable, mysterious work of the Spirit of God defies human comprehension. The Spirit lives within us on good days and bad days, during thankful times and sinful scenarios, and the Spirit interprets our prayers continually. That is certainly much more than even the best of us deserve. God—this Triune God—loves people with everything that makes Him the God of heaven, the Savior of the world, and the guiding Spirit of humankind.

As the redeemed of the Lord, we can see that behind the above scriptures is the indescribable and unexplainable love of the God who will do anything and everything to secure the salvation of those He loves. Love motivated God to send Jesus; love prompted Jesus to leave heaven and willingly die on that cross; love drives the Holy Spirit to live within us to steadfastly guide us. Love is behind everything that God does and is. God extends His love to all people, and God desires that all people come to know His love. God does not want to leave anyone behind.

As Christians who desire to be like our God, we must take on this quality of love for people. It is not a matter of whether or not people deserve love; it is simply that God loves people—the good and the bad, the beautiful and the ugly, the rich and the poor, the deserving and the undeserving, the lost and the saved. God loves people; as His children, we are called to love people as well.

Because of the great love that our God has for all people, I have written this book to call the redeemed of the Lord to arms. We already know that we are engaged in a war—not a war for land or power or greed, or even democracy; we are engaged in a war for souls. Our arms are not ships or airplanes or tanks or guns. Our arms are prayer and prayer and prayer and prayer, for the enemy we fight against is Satan—a formidable enemy indeed!

As I share with you, in the next few chapters, what I have learned by praying for the lost, I ask that you consider joining with me and others in bringing the lost souls of this world to the throne room of our God. I realize that many people already are in the habit of praying for the lost. But now I ask that all of us extend the boundaries of who and what we pray for, and I challenge all of us to regularly take to God an individual, a group of people or an issue that is currently not on our prayer list.

Please give this request prayerful consideration as you read the next few chapters. I will revisit this request again at the end of the book.

JESUS

Lessons I Have Learned

✤ ✤ ✤

The Father of the Fatal

❖ ❖ ❖

*May the Lord God Almighty,
who is the Lion of the tribe of Judah
and the Lord of the Heavenly Host,
protect us from him who seeks to destroy
all that is good and right and wholesome.*

If we are going to join hands (and prayers) in battle against Satan, prudence demands that we know our enemy. As a matter of fact, that *was* the title for this chapter: "Know the Enemy." Originally, I wanted to collect some battle statistics on some of the major wars over the course of recent history. I thought perhaps some numbers concerning how many soldiers were injured or killed in World War I or II or in the Gulf War or even the war in Iraq would help to underscore the gravity of going to war—both physical war and spiritual war. I even called my brother, who has an eighteen-year career in the air force, and asked him a few questions about knowing the enemy. I also considered reading a couple of books on spiritual warfare to see what others had to say about doing battle with the enemy.

As I began to head in this direction, though, I sensed I was not going down the right path, so I changed direction. Now, there is nothing wrong with studying one's enemy. In the heat of battle, knowing the possible methods and moves of the enemy is invaluable. However, our enemy is someone we already know. The face behind the hurt, behind the bondage, behind the lostness of humanity is the angel who was cast out of heaven: Satan.

Paul tells us in Ephesians 6:12 that "our struggle is not against flesh and blood, but against the rulers, against the authorities, against the powers of this dark world and against the spiritual forces of evil in the heavenly realms." [5]

The leader of these forces is none other than Satan. Actually, his leadership abilities are beyond compare— and his hate for God and humankind is without end. He is an enemy whose thirst for destruction is unquenchable. He is an enemy who does not play by the rules, who uses any and all weaknesses against his foes. He is an enemy to respect. And though his destiny is hell, his intention is to take as many with him as possible. No, we must not underestimate this five-star general, this hater of righteousness, this destroyer of good, this seducer of souls.

Perhaps Satan's greatest joy (and God's greatest grief) is that people are so easily seduced by him. In John 8:44, Jesus calls Satan "a liar and the father of lies." [6] The capacity people have for swallowing a lie is amazing. How many times have we been taken in by a lie? Satan lies to us in innumerable ways. He seduces people—both the saved and the unsaved—by whispering to us that we have the right to feel the way we feel and think the thoughts we think, even when those feelings and thoughts run contrary to God's word. He whispers to us that we need this or that, and we should do anything necessary to obtain the desired object—be it person or thing. Satan is the father of the fatal: the fatal passion of hate that assassinates people, both in body or character; the fatal idea of revenge at all costs; the fatal mistake that destroys personal integrity; the fatal rendezvous that comes at the expense of the marriage; the fatal apathy or arrogance that turns man or woman from God.

Some of you may be thinking, "Yes, Satan is the rogue that he has been painted to be here, but we have a choice"—and we do. We do not have to listen to Satan. We do not have to succumb to his temptations. But we all do, don't we? He is shrewd, relentless, and powerful.

Do you remember the story of the transfiguration in Matthew 17? When Jesus came down from the mountain, He was met by His disciples and a crowd of people. In the crowd was a father who had brought his demon-possessed son to be cured, but the disciples were unable to cast the spirit out of the boy. Naturally, Jesus dispatched the spirit forthwith. Later, the disciples asked Jesus why they couldn't cast the spirit out. Jesus told them in verse 21 (a footnote in some translations) that "this kind does not go out except by prayer and fasting." [7] The demonic forces of hell are formidable. We are not able to deal with Satan and his demons on our own. Adam and Eve found that out in the garden, Jesus's disciples found that out in Matthew 17, and we discover that every time we sin. Our battle with the hellish host is in the heavenly realms, and our weapons are heavenly as well—faith in a God we know is more powerful than they and prayer to a God who guides and protects the ones He loves. Satan, the demon who so eagerly tempts us to numerous fatal mistakes, may only be thwarted by the power of the Lord God Almighty.

Another indication of Satan's power is in Matthew 12, when the Pharisees accuse Jesus of casting out demons by Beelzebub. Jesus's response is, "How can anyone enter a strong man's house and carry off his possessions unless he first ties up the strong man? Then he can rob his house" (verse 29).[8] Prayer in the name of Jesus Christ gives us the ability to bind the strong man, to silence the seducer, to rout the father of the fatal. We must remember that against Satan and his attempts to add all of us to his fatality list, there is a weapon he cannot withstand: prayer in the name of the Son of God! One of the most amazing aspects of being a Christian is that I can call upon the name of Jesus Christ, and Satan has no choice but to take a hike!

When was the last time you saw a movie and wanted to stand up to clap and cheer? We all know the feeling. The movie was so good, so stirring, struck such a chord with the heart and spirit that we wanted to jump up, clap, and cheer. The last time that feeling came over me was when I saw Mel Gibson's *The Passion of the Christ*.

In many ways, and at many times during the movie, that would not seem to be the appropriate reaction. There are so many scenes that are heart-wrenching—the betrayal, the scenes before the high priest, the beating, the walk to Calvary, the crucifixion. But my favorite scene in the whole movie is right at the beginning, in the garden. Do you remember? Jesus is lying prostrate on the ground praying. Satan appears, and from under his robe comes a snake. I hate snakes! I wasn't even sure I could watch the scene; I usually close my eyes when there's anything to do with snakes, but I didn't this time. The snake slithers and hisses its way toward Jesus. I wanted to scream, "Watch out!" But Jesus stands up, looks at Satan, and with one crushing blow from his heel, He smashes the head of the serpent.[9] I wanted to jump out of my skin! I wanted to jump up and clap and yell and dance! I was beyond happy; I was exultant! And while I didn't do all that physically, you better believe my spirit was doing it. It took several minutes for my heart to stop racing and my mind to settle back to the movie. Every time I watch that movie—which is once a year on Good Friday—my reaction is the same. I want to jump out of my seat and clap and yell and dance! The foe has been defeated; the enemy has lost his power; the strong man has been overcome. Satan has lost!

Until the time comes, however, when Jesus removes Satan permanently from our presence, we must remember that Satan is a formidable foe whose sole purpose is to bring death and destruction where God would give life and abundance. Indeed, Satan may be happiest when some temptation overtakes the free will of a man or a woman. We must not, we dare not, underestimate this enemy whom we fight in this battle for souls. He will use any and all means to assault us. His attacks are constant, ruthless, and downright dirty, but we must remember the garden.

We must remember that the Son of God, our Savior and Lord, the One who is preparing our home and who sits at the right hand of the Father in heaven, has smashed the head of the serpent. We must remember that when we pray in the mighty name of the Son of God that name gives us power over the forces of hell. The war wages on until the Father decides there will be no more battles; but, rest assured, the victory belongs to heaven!

Eyes Wide Open

✤ ✤ ✤

*Give us, oh Father, a clear perception
of the deceitful ways of the evil one.
Protect us from his snares
and keep our feet on righteous and holy ground.*

Along with coming to a better understanding of the power of Satan, my years of praying for the lost also have taught me to be prepared. Going into battle with one's guard down is the hallmark of a foolish soldier. Becoming lackadaisical about one's surroundings and purpose invites disaster, and, as is true of all battle situations, even the soldier who is alert and prepared can still be injured or killed. We would be foolish indeed to think that Satan will ignore people who commit to pray for lost souls. On the contrary, committing to pray for others will most assuredly come with risks. Satan will not idly sit by and watch his kingdom of darkness decrease while God's kingdom of light increases. In fact, praying may come with a price. I do not know the exact approach Satan will use to stop people from praying, but I am confident he will march out in full force to meet the attack.

Satan is conniving, ruthless, and patient—very patient. He is the master at setting a trap and waiting to let all the individual pieces fall into place—even if that means waiting for months or years. We see this all the time as believers and nonbelievers alike succumb to a variety of temptations. Adultery and embezzlement are two common examples. In these two instances, we may ask the following question: was the desire to take that person or that money instantaneous? Perhaps, but most likely not. Satan is more than willing to wait a few months or a few years (what's that in the scope of eternity?) to allow time, desire, and opportunity to bring about often fatal ruin.

Satan also is the author of "busyness"—a word that could be a synonym for our culture today. I often hear Christians and non-Christians alike speaking of their busy lives: always appointments to keep, children to take and pick up, overtime at work, endless hours of grocery shopping and housecleaning. I am not suggesting these activities should not be done. What I am suggesting is that our culture seems to glorify activity, for activity suggests purpose. Perhaps Satan has patiently brought American culture to the brink of physical and spiritual collapse because of its busyness. The irony, of course, is that our busyness may be spent participating in the good instead of participating in the best. It is a good thing to expose our children to sports, the arts, the companionship of other children. It is a good thing to bring home extra money. It is a good thing to have groceries in the house and a clean bathroom. Do we, however, spend as much time at Sunday dinner around the table with family and friends? Family devotionals, so we do not start or end the day without God? Bible study, to learn about the God who loves us? Prayer, that will mature us into the people God wants us to be? The truth may be this: if Satan can keep us busy doing the good, then we have less time to participate in the best. Perhaps Satan's most powerful weapon against today's world is busyness.

Whether Satan tempts us with some devilish sin or keeps us busy from morning to midnight, we must understand that he is committed to do anything and everything to keep us from praying for the lost. We must all realize that to be prayer warriors means to come under attack from the host of hell, no matter what form that attack may take. We must, therefore, enter this battle for souls with our eyes wide open.

If this sounds a bit scary, it is. Satan comes to the war equipped to do battle. He comes prepared to do whatever it takes to keep unbelievers from coming into contact with the God of heaven, the Father of life, the Lover of all souls. He comes prepared to stop as many believers' prayers as possible from ascending to the throne of God. He will tempt and confuse us. He will make us question and doubt. He will do all that is necessary to stop these prayers.

Here's an example from my own life of coming under attack from the enemy. The weekly prayer group that I mentioned earlier consisted of four women—two staff members and two faculty members. When certain departments on campus were realigned, several people, including one of the staff members in the prayer group, submitted their resignations. A few months later, twelve to fifteen people were laid off due to financial cutbacks. Among them was the other staff member in our prayer group—and myself.

I clearly remember the day the two of us lost our jobs. I received an e-mail from the academic dean requesting that I meet with her and the academic vice president after my class. As soon as I read the e-mail, I knew I had lost my job. I called the other staff member and told her about the e-mail and what I thought it meant. She said she had also received one from her boss, and her meeting was in ten minutes. We both knew we had lost our jobs.

Both of us had been part of this prayer group for eight years and the other two women for five years. Satan certainly may have taken advantage of the financial situation at the college to dissolve our prayer group. We don't understand why things turned out the way they did, but I do know that God is faithful, and He never abandons His children. I do know that God's ways are not my ways, and from confusion and disillusionment, He gives peace and purpose and opportunity. I do know that God is love, and whatever damage Satan may inflict on people who pray, that damage cannot separate us from God's love, presence, care, and guidance.

Yes, praying may come with a price. It may be something as difficult as losing a job or something as simple as losing a few hours' sleep. This side of the coin may bring some confusion and bewilderment. It will certainly have its moments of doubt and weakness. The other side of the coin, however, offers something invaluable. It is the unfathomable, priceless gift of being allowed to pray in the presence of the Almighty, feeling His love and strength and power as we join with Him to bring His message to the lost, the lonely, the deceived, and the desperate.

We must come to this battle for souls with our eyes wide open, aware that Satan is real and that he operates in this world for the purpose of destroying both the saved and the unsaved. We must come with our eyes wide open to the possibility, and probably certainty, of attack. But we must also come with our eyes wide open to the assurances of God, and with an understanding that any price on this temporary earth is worth paying if it saves just one person from the clutches of Satan and an eternity in hell.

✦ ✦ ✦

Heart Wide Open

✦ ✦ ✦

❖ ❖ ❖

Oh God of all compassion,
may we see this lost and dying world
through Your eyes of love and mercy and grace.
May we extend to others
what You so completely and freely bestow upon us—
Your unconditional love.

❖ ❖ ❖

The *New Oxford American Dictionary* defines compassion as "sympathetic pity and concern for the sufferings or misfortunes of others." I always thought I had a compassionate heart—at least as much as the next person, and perhaps a little more, considering that I am a Christian—but God had something to teach me about compassion as I continued to pray for lost souls.

Essentially, I have made a lifetime commitment to God to pray for three groups of people. The first group I've already mentioned: Muslims. However, my intent from the moment the idea for this book was born was to leave the "for whom" people pray between those individuals and God. Therefore, I will not be divulging the specifics of the other two groups of people for whom I pray. Instead, I will title the second group "The Misguided" and the third group, "The Lost." I will come back to The Misguided later.

I thought of praying for The Lost long before I actually began praying for them—several months before, in fact. I was still working at the college the first time I remember thinking of this group. During one of our weekly meetings, my prayer group was discussing The Lost and the adverse effects their lifestyles have on people. The group prayed that day for these people, and I thought to myself that perhaps I should add this group to my own prayer list. I had often thought I should have three groups to pray for—I just like the number—but I didn't really want to pray for these people, so I dismissed the idea and continued to ask God to lay on my heart the third group for whom He would like me to pray.

Several weeks later, when I was with the prayer group again, the thought came to me to pray for The Lost. I ignored it. On the way back to my office after the meeting, I told God that I just did not want to pray for these people.

I mentioned a myriad of issues and groups that needed prayer, and certainly I could pray for one of these.

A few more weeks went by, and the same thing happened again. The prayer group met, I thought of The Lost, and on the way back to my office, I told God that I just did not want to pray for them.

My apartment complex is close to a ten-mile-long bike path through a beautiful wooded area, and I often walk the path to pray. I was out walking and praying one day for the other two groups, and I thought of The Lost again. I was really quite emphatic to God this time. I remember saying, "No! I do not want to pray for these people."

Well ... you can imagine God's response to this continued refusal. Allow me to offer some advice here. It does not pay to be stubborn with God! He can last a lot longer than we can. A few weeks later, I was out walking and praying for my two groups, and The Lost came to mind again. This time, in a rather exasperated tone, I said, "OK. I'll pray for them. But why me? I don't really want to pray for them because I find their particular offense rather distasteful. Do I really have to be thinking about that all the time? I'm sure there are plenty of other Christians who would pray for these people. Are You sure You don't want to ask them?"

I began to feel that I was indeed the one being asked, so I reluctantly began praying for The Lost.

Those who have done any amount of praying know that the person who is most affected by the praying is often the person *doing* the praying. This has certainly been the case for me. Though I began praying for The Lost with exasperation and reluctance, I now pray for them with compassion and tenderness. As time went on and I continued to pray for these people, my hard, stubborn heart began to change (surprise! surprise!). On this year long prayer journey for The Lost, I have learned much about myself, about God, and about compassion. I learned that a compassionate heart is a heart that is wide open, able to genuinely care about and love people—all kinds of people. To be brutally honest with myself, as far as The Lost are concerned, I had conceived notions about and a closed heart to their situations and circumstances. I had fallen into the hard-hearted trap of "Let someone else care about them; let someone else help them; let someone else pray for them." My heart needed an airing out, so to speak, or at least another room added on to it.

At first, the only thing I could see was disgusting behavior and habits. I saw lives that were "turned on" to Satan and "turned off" to God. I saw people in rebellion to God, people who didn't care about Him or about following His ways, people who didn't care about His existence—who probably didn't even believe in His existence. I did not hate these people or wish them harm. I simply did not want to think about them or their sordid behaviors. For the first several weeks—months, even—of praying for this group, all I saw was the *sin* of these people, and not the *people*. Now, I see the people—and my heart aches for them. Oh, I know some of them will continue in their rebellion, caring nothing for God and being totally duped by Satan, yet thinking they are in complete control of their lives. But I now see faces that express fear and entrapment and hopelessness—faces that say, "How did I get into this?" or "I can never find my way out of this," or "I just don't matter to anyone."

During my years as an English teacher, one of the courses I taught regularly was Composition B. The course is much like an introduction to literature. One of the genres of literature we read is drama. My all-time favorite play— and the one I taught the most—is Lorraine Hansberry's *A Raisin in the Sun*. If you have never read it, please do—or at least see the film version with Sidney Poitier. The play is about a poor African-American family living on Chicago's South Side during the 1950s. When the father dies, the mother receives a $10,000 insurance check in the mail. The grown son loses most of the money in a bad business deal. Obviously, the family is devastated. The grown sister now despises her brother, but Mama has something to say about that. Allow me to pick up in midstream:

> MAMA. Yes—I taught you that. Me and your daddy. But I thought I taught you something else too... I thought I taught you to love him.
>
> BENEATHA. Love him? There is nothing left to love.
>
> MAMA. There is always something left to love. And if you ain't learned that, you ain't learned nothing. Have you cried for that boy today? I don't mean for yourself and for the family 'cause we lost the money. I mean for him; what he been through and what it done to him. Child, when do you think is the time to love somebody the most; when they done good and made things easy for everybody? Well then, you ain't through learning—because that ain't the time at all. It's when he's at his lowest and can't believe in hisself 'cause the world done whipped him so. When you starts measuring somebody, measure him right, child, measure him right. [10]

I can't help but think of these amazing lines when I think of The Lost. To me, The Lost are choosing to do something as stupid and reckless as the son in this play, but, unlike in the play, these people are not throwing money away—they're throwing away their eternal souls. In the play, the son refuses to let go of the idea of this business deal, but as a reader, I know he is being taken in. Likewise, The Lost refuse to let go of a sinful lifestyle, but as a Christian, I know they have been taken in by Satan and are sacrificing their heavenly home with God.

Mama's words cut me to the quick. When did I think it was time to love these people? When did I think it was time to pray for these people? Satan has led these people to a low and sinful place, and Satan's places are always dark and deceptive and death-filled. These people needed—still need—my prayers. It's not about me. It's not about how distasteful or disgusting or sinful I think the actions of these people are. It's about something much bigger: the redemption of lost souls. It's about the God who created all of us and loves all of us. It's about the God who loves sinners (myself included) so much that He chose the cross to save us from those sins. My sins have been washed away by the blood of my Savior, and I am now a child of the loving Father in heaven. But these people do not know the Savior or the Father or their love. How can I not pray for these lost souls? How can I not plead with our Heavenly Father to bring about circumstances in their lives that will put them in contact with the blood of Jesus? How can I not bring these people, who Jesus loves and for whom He died, to the throne room of the Lord God Almighty on a regular basis?

Along with educating my own heart, I had the privilege of learning a little more about the heart of God. I am astonished at His patience and acceptance. I have always known that God is a patient God; after all, look how long He has been putting up with human beings! But I think that God's patience has more impact when the experience is personal. I stand amazed at God's quiet patience with me in the light of two specific situations associated with The Lost.

The first situation is the length of time it took me to finally begin praying. Roughly eight to ten months passed from the time I first had the thought to the time I actually said the first prayer. During those months, God patiently kept bringing this group of people back into my mind. Perhaps this was a small-scale "Jonah situation" for me. I did not run away, but I certainly refused to listen. Though I did not despise these people as Jonah did the Ninevites, I certainly was disgusted with them. Fortunately, I was not swallowed by a big fish since I live nowhere near the ocean (I do occasionally, though, keep an eye on that little brook that runs by the bike path!).

God's patience is so wonderful. He patiently and gently (seems like those two always go together, don't they?) kept knocking on the chambers of my heart by shining His light into the darkness He saw there. As I continued praying for The Lost, I began to think about flesh-and-blood people, not a faceless mass of humanity. I began thinking about how life's circumstances can be overwhelming at times, and how Satan takes such artful aim at us when we become overwhelmed by life. Without God's guidance and protection, these people stand ripe for the slaughter by the prowling lion of hell. Oh, I know people have to pay the consequences for their own sinful decisions and actions, but isn't that why Jesus came to earth—to save us from eternal consequences? For the first time in my life, I had an eye-opening (or rather heart-opening) glimpse of the depth and breadth of a God who so deeply loves all the people He created. His gentle patience brought light into a shadowy and dark place in my heart that I didn't even know was there. This great God knows us so much better than we know ourselves! His light brought a new vision, a clear vision of what it means to love and to pray for the lost.

The second situation that so clearly reveals God's patience with me was my blunt refusals to pray for these people. God said pray; I said no. I look back on those refusals now and think, "Debbie. What on earth were you thinking?" Loving Father that He is, God patiently waited for my heart to hear His small, still voice. Sometimes I wonder that I did. I was so sure that I couldn't be the one to pray for these people; after all, they left this dirty taste in my mouth (that should have been my first clue). I didn't know for whom I thought I should be praying, but I remember not having any clear picture of any group or situation in my mind (that should have been my second clue). God was answering my prayer all along; I just wasn't listening. With exasperation, I finally began to pray. It's amazing what God can do with the human heart, even one that is so "off the target"!

Through this experience, I have learned that compassion is a gift from God, and His compassion is as big as the sky and as deep as the ocean. I no longer view The Lost through the lens of their sins. In some small way, I have begun to see them through the eyes of our all-compassionate Father—and at times this brings me to tears.

I see people who are trapped in a lifestyle and are not sure how to get out of it. I ask God to guide their footsteps and lead them to people who can show them a path away from this sin.

I see people who have hopelessness etched on their faces. I ask God to give them the strength to continue on and somehow open their hearts and minds to Jesus—the only sure hope for all of us.

I see people who are being used by Satan and by others, who question if there is anyone out there who truly cares for them. I know the answer to that question is a resounding *yes!* So I ask God to somehow shine the light of His love into their lives and lead these bruised, used, and battered people to a group of His people who can see beyond the sin to the souls who are lonely, life-scarred, and lost.

What I used to see were people who offended me, who stood in open rebellion against God and what He has said is right and good and holy. And though The Lost are still in rebellion against God, I now see people, not just the sin. Jesus said in Luke 19:10 that He has come "to seek and to save what was lost." [11] What is lost is not always a pretty sight. It has often been twisted and hardened by Satan. The Lost have been deceived by Satan, and many are so consumed with their way of life that they would never think of changing who they are or what they do. These are the people we sometimes think are beyond reach, those whose hearts are made of stone. I ask God to look into these hearts and continue to shine His light into the lives of those He knows can be changed. John 1:5 tells us, "The light shines in the darkness, and the darkness has not overcome it" (New Revised Standard Version).[12] As this scripture suggests, the heart of stone *can* be reached.

To see the saving grace of the Savior in action, I recommend the movie *The Scarlet and the Black,* with Gregory Peck and Christopher Plummer. It is based on the true story of the Nazi occupation of Rome during World War II.[13] Just as compelling are the stories of two tax collectors named Matthew and Zacchaeus, who gave up their lucrative profession to follow Jesus; and a zealot named Simon, who gave up street marauding and murder to follow Jesus—not to mention an overzealous Pharisee named Saul of Tarsus, whose favorite pastime was jailing and killing Christians. God's light and love and compassion are steady and sure, piercing dark and evil hearts in this world in order to bring truth and love into these lives—while also piercing the heart of one woman to teach her the difference between the sin and the sinner.

At the end of the movie *Wide Awake*, Joshua, the main character, is reading his end-of-term essay to his fifth-grade class. It has been a rough school year for Joshua; among other difficulties, his beloved grandfather died. He writes in his essay, "Before this year, people I loved lived forever. I spent this year looking for something and wound up seeing everything around me. It was like I was asleep before and finally woke up. Know what? I'm wide awake now." [14]

I feel so much like Joshua. I was asleep to the peril of this group of people, but God has awakened my heart. Through His patience, love, and compassion, I now have a heart that is wide awake. I will never be the same. I will compassionately and faithfully pray for The Lost until the Lord takes me home, when I'll get to see the God who gave me a heart wide open.

Praying on the Edge

*Praises be to the One
who sits on the throne of heaven.
May He grant to us visions of His limitless love
and glory and power.*

A final lesson I have learned while praying for people who are lost is that I can enter the throne room of God with confidence. I believe that God is hearing my prayers and trust that He is answering them, though I do not see the results of that for which I pray. I have no association with any of the groups I regularly take to God, but I have discovered what it means to "pray on the edge." By this I mean that over the years God has greatly enhanced my view of the concept of coming to Him with boldness. Let me explain.

Shortly after I began praying for Muslims, I felt the need to ask for the salvation of a certain number of people. I did not do this because I thought God wanted me to; I did this for me. At that time, I needed something concrete to help me pray. I needed to visualize a group of people who were being touched by my prayers. I do not believe God is into number games. This was just a way for me to journey down this prayer road with God and with these people. I felt I needed a number I could conceptualize, so I chose four thousand. There is a little story behind that number.

If you haven't already guessed, I love to watch movies. I wish I could say that I used to teach film appreciation so that I would have a good reason for watching so many different types of movies, but I didn't. I just love watching movies! And I enjoy watching them more than once. Good movies are like good books; it's difficult to catch everything on the first go-round. Soon after I began praying for the Muslims, I re-watched the movie I mentioned earlier, *The Scarlet and the Black*. The number four thousand is mentioned in the movie (but I don't want to give anything else away, so please, go watch this movie!). So I came to God with this number, and for several months I prayed for the redemption of four thousand Muslims.

At first, four thousand people seemed like a lot. Actually, I was impressed with that number. I thought, "Wow! I'm praying for four thousand people." I had never prayed for the salvation of so many before. Eventually, though, the smallness of the number nagged at me. I remember praying, "God, I feel the number is too small. I'm not trying to play number games with You, but I really sense this number needs to take a big leap." I decided to add a zero to it and arrived at forty thousand.

Ephesians 3:20–21 states, "Now to Him who is able to do immeasurably more than all we ask or imagine, according to His power that is at work within us, to Him be glory in the church and in Christ Jesus throughout all generations, for ever and ever! Amen." [15] I am convinced that so many times I just think too small. Just what exactly is "immeasurably more" than what I can imagine? I can imagine a lot! If I believe I serve a God who has the ability to do anything I can dream of (within the confines of His will, that is), then all limits are off. God is not restricted in power or purpose. He is not held back by lack of resources or knowledge or ability or wisdom. He is omnipotent, omnipresent, and omniscient. In a sense, though, He is restricted by my view of who He is. If my view of God is small, then my God is small. Truth be known, I both believe and don't believe that God is restricted. I sincerely believe God can reach beyond my limited view of who He is and do marvelous deeds. Perhaps the being who is really restricted, who really gets placed into a box, is me. In this funny little journey of numbers, I believe God has begun to collapse the sides of the box I am in when it comes to my perception of just what He is willing and able to do.

For many months I prayed this number, forty thousand. But I didn't want to get lost in the numbers, so I began picturing individual people searching for God. I began picturing God helping this man or that woman to find Him. This gave me a sense of personal contact with this large group of people who were unknown to me, but who were intimately known by God. After several months of this, that nagging, too-small number feeling came back … and I thought, "You have got to be kidding!" After all, forty thousand is a pretty large group of people, but there it was—that nagging thought that I needed to go higher. So I decided that if the feeling of not praying for a large enough number of people was going to keep coming back around, I was going to go all out this time! If I was going to pray to the Divine about the redemption of lost souls, then I was going to go for a number that I thought would challenge the Divine (if that is possible). Practically on the heels of that thought, I increased the number to four million. Now, I cannot possibly keep track of four million people. I can't even conceive of four million people. But I know God can. From the day I began praying for four million people, I have believed God is totally aware of who these people are and can work in their individual life situations to soften their hearts to believe and accept the saving message of Jesus Christ.

You probably think I stopped there … but I didn't. I took one more gigantic leap of absurdity. I went from the outrageous to the ridiculous, and I believe with all my heart God is acting on behalf of my prayers. I did not experience that nagging feeling to increase the number of people I was praying for, but one day I went online and discovered that the worldwide population of the Islamic faith is roughly 1.3 billion people. I looked up the number out of curiosity and was rather awed by it. I didn't realize the number was that high. I had a passing thought to pray for half, but then I told myself, "Have you totally lost your mind? You can't conceive of four million. How can you pray for a number that you can't even imagine?" The thought simmered in the back of my mind for several days until I finally realized that this is not about the number. It's about the salvation of people for whom I have chosen to pray. It's about having faith and trust and confidence that God will respond to those prayers, even if the number I carry to Him is utterly ridiculous. It's about believing that God knows and loves each one of those individuals, for He doesn't see a mass of humanity. He sees the individual sheep without its shepherd, the individual child without its Father, the individual soul without its God. I have no idea how God will work in the lives of so many people (that's not my job, anyway), but for the past year or so, I have been asking God for the redemption of half a billion Muslims.

At first read, this may sound like an absurd little numbers game with the Almighty. Let me assure you that that has not been the case. From the very beginning, I have been dead serious about the number of people I take to God in prayer. I pray believing He hears my prayers and is dead serious Himself about answering them. Starting with the concrete visualization of four thousand people and ending four or five years later with the unfathomable number of more than half a billion has had a profound impact on my idea of approaching God with boldness. Jesus said in John 12:32 that He would draw all men to Him, and in Matthew 19:26 He reminds us that "[w]ith man this [saving people] is impossible, but with God all things are possible." [16] As an English teacher, I often told my students to avoid all-inclusive terms in their papers. As human beings, how could we possibly know the ramifications of *all* situations and circumstances? However, when Jesus says He can draw *all* men to Him and says that God can do *all* things, perhaps I need to sit up and take notice.

I know that there are many people in the Islamic world who are responding to the Gospel. I feel honored to join my voice with so many others who are praying and working to bring the message of Jesus Christ to the Muslim nations. May all of us who pray for lost souls do so with confidence and boldness, believing that God will answer our prayers "immeasurably more" than what any of us can imagine!

Closing Remarks

✤ ✤ ✤

Answering the Call to Pray

❖ ❖ ❖

*Bless us, Eternal Father, as we, Your redeemed,
carry to Your throne room those who have been overpowered
by the prowling lion of hell.
Extend to these lost souls
the healing power of Your presence
and the salvation found only
in the power of the cross.*

I said the purpose of this book was to specifically ask each individual Christian to open his or her heart to a commitment to pray for an individual or a group of people or a specific issue. I would now like to revisit that request.

Let me say, first of all, that I know I am not the only person praying for the three groups of people that I mentioned. I realize that my voice is joining other voices who pray for these lost souls. The hearts of many Christians are touched by the lost souls of this world, and many Christians throughout the centuries have prayed and become missionaries because of their love and concern for the lost. I simply want to ask anyone who reads this book to pray, along with others, for the lost souls of this world, whoever they may be.

In this closing section, there are three aspects about praying for lost souls that I would like to address. First, for whom do I pray? As I mentioned earlier, I have felt that the "for whom" I am asking people to pray should be left between those individuals and God. Some of you may already have a stirring in your hearts for a specific person, group, or issue. That was the way it was with me and The Misguided. Soon after I began praying for the Muslims, I began praying for this second group. My heart had been drawn to them, and I occasionally prayed for them already. Some of you, on the other hand, may not know for whom to pray. You may not feel an attraction to any specific person, group, or issue. In this case, may I suggest that you ask God to lay on your heart those for whom He would want you to pray, as I did. Hopefully, you will be a better listener than I was, but if you pray believing that God will make it clear to you those for whom He wants you to pray, He will.

Next, I would like to mention "how often" to pray. This is really up to you. I would like to share with you, however, how often I pray for my groups. The truth is that it is quite irregular. I have not set up a specific prayer schedule. By this,

I mean I have not done anything such as on Mondays, pray for group number one; on Wednesdays, pray for group number two; on Fridays, pray for group number three. I remember trying this at first, but it simply did not work for me. Usually, I pray for each group at least once a week, but there have been times when even that has not happened. There have been times when many days, even weeks, have gone by, and I haven't prayed for one group or another. Then there are those times when I have concentrated on one group and prayed for that group several days running. A couple of times I have prayed for all three groups in one day. Occasionally, I feel a burden on my heart for one group or another, and when that happens, I pray numerous times in one day for that group. As you can see, I have no specific pattern that I follow. I simply pray regularly for my groups. My "regular" may be different from your "regular." Pray as often as you feel the need. I have no doubt that God and your own heart will lead you to what works best for you.

The last aspect to address is "how long." My commitment has been a lifetime one from the very beginning. I remember each time that I decided to pray for a specific group, I told God that I wanted to pray for this group on a regular basis until the day I died. But just because I have made a lifetime commitment does not mean that everyone else should. Perhaps some people would like to pray for one group for three months, six months, or a year. Some people may want to pray for a different person, group, or issue each year. Actually, the length of time can be as various as we are. But whatever time commitment we make, I believe we must take the commitment seriously, since God expects us to fulfill our commitments to Him.

In drawing this request to a close, there are a couple of other thoughts I want to share. One is the idea of the wounded warrior. Sometimes in battle, the most frightening and most surprising fighter is the one who has been wounded. There is now nothing to lose in putting forth that final, supreme effort to attack the enemy. I remember clearly this moment in my own prayer life. I had been wounded: I had lost my job and my car, and I had no idea what I was going to do next. A day or two after I lost my job I was walking the bike path and praying about my situation. I was crying, and I remember being frightened of the situation in which I had found myself. But I also remember being overwhelmed with a steely resolve that no matter what Satan put in my path, I would not stop praying. I'm not really looking for fierce battles and wounds, but the question I want Satan to ask is: "Why can I not keep her down?" My prayer goal is to get up one more time than I have been knocked down.

Next, I would like to suggest a short list of books on prayer. There are many more besides these, and family, friends, and preachers are often a good source to discovering other excellent books on prayer. Here are a few titles that I have in my library:

- *The Imitation of Christ,* by Thomas à Kempis (this is actually a devotional book, but I could not give a list of books without including it)
- *The Essentials of Prayer*, by E.M. Bounds
- *Prayer*, by Richard J. Foster.

I also recently purchased *Get Off Your Knees and Pray*, by Sheila Walsh, and *Prayer: Does It Make A Difference?*, by Philip Yancey.

Though there are many good books worth reading on this subject, the most important activity is praying itself. Do not feel compelled to read even one book before the actual praying begins. God is the greatest director of our hearts, and I have no doubt that not only will He guide His people to those who need prayer, but He also will guide our hearts to those books that will touch our minds and spirits.

There is one final thought and one final movie I would like to mention. In *The Lord of the Rings: The Fellowship of the Ring*, Gandalf, Frodo, and the others are traveling through the mines of Moria. They have come to a place where they must decide to take one of three paths available to them. Gandalf is the decision-maker in the group, and while he is trying to decide which path they should take, he and Frodo have a short discussion about the ring:

> FRODO: I wish the ring had never come to me. I wish none of this had happened.
>
> GANDALF: So do all who live to see such times, but that is not for them to decide. All we have to decide is what to do with the time that is given to us. There are other forces at work in this world, Frodo, besides the one of evil. [17]

Sometimes the evil in our world seems so overwhelming. Sometimes it appears that Satan is winning. As Gandalf reminds Frodo, though, there *are* other forces at work in this world besides the one of evil. Our God is at work. He has always been at work. As long as this world endures, He will continue to be at work. He still sits on the throne of heaven, forever in control, forever offering His love. And His love is the one thing in this world that cannot be stopped or defeated. His love is the one thing that has the power to transform people, and that which transforms people also transforms the world.

As His redeemed, we are at work with Him. Because of His transforming power in us, we now live with eyes made new to see the hurting; with hands made useful to help the needy; with hearts made tender to love the unlovable. As

His son or daughter, please consider working with Him in one more area and make a commitment to pray for a specific person, group, or issue that is not currently on your prayer list.

Heaven and hell we can only guess at, but one thing is certain: heaven contains the presence of God, and hell does not. Eternal separation from the presence of the Divine will be much more than mere words can express. If an entire lifetime of praying saves one soul, *just one soul*, then it is worth every prayer, every struggle, every tear, every moment spent!

❖ ❖ ❖

Give Praise

❖ ❖ ❖

The Lord God Almighty is known by many names.
For several months now, I have wanted to close this book
by writing something that details these names.
My purpose is not only to praise the God who is all these
names, but also to encourage and comfort us as we pray
for those who do not yet know the absolutely
amazing and profound God whom we serve.

❖ ❖ ❖

To the Lord God Almighty who sits on the throne of heaven: praises be to Him who is holy, perfect, and altogether righteous. May the angels join us in adoring the Lord God Jehovah, He who is self-existent, the Yahweh of both Old and New covenants. May the blessed Elohim of heaven be our might and strength as we walk this journey called life. May we forever rely on El Shaddai, the God who is all-sufficient. Praises be to Adonai, the Lord of your life, the Lord of my life, the Lord of all.

May we continually proclaim the everlasting love of Jehovah-Shammah, the Lord who is there, who has always been there, who will always be there. Blessed be our God who never abandons those He loves.

Sing praises to Jehovah-M'Kaddesh, the Lord who sanctifies, and to Jehovah-Tsidkenu, the Lord our righteousness. For He was willing, even before time began, to offer His Son as a sacrifice for our sins that we, for all eternity, may delight in the company of His presence.

Give glory to God Almighty, the One who sends rain on the just and the unjust, the One who supplies His creation with all its needs, the One who grants to us all good things, for He is Jehovah-Jireh, the Lord who provides.

Let the sick of body, the sick of mind, and the sick of spirit shout to Jehovah-Rophe, the Lord who heals, for He is not unaware of our diseases nor incapable of healing us.

Let us all cry out to Jehovah-Rohi, the Lord our shepherd, who throughout our lives leads us to pastures green and good.

Blessed be Jehovah-Nissi, the Lord our banner, who commands the angelic armies for His good purposes.

May we always put our trust in Jehovah-Sabaoth, the Lord of Hosts, whom Satan, in the end, will not be able to withstand.

Glory and honor to Jehovah-Shalom, the Lord our peace, who in times of calm and chaos comforts us with the tranquility of His voice and presence.

Praises be to El Elyon, Abhir, Kadosh, and El-Olam, the Most High, the Mighty One, the Holy One, the Everlasting God.

May He who sits in the shadow of the Most High, the Holy One of God, the only begotten Son of the Father, the Lion of the tribe of Judah, and the root and offspring of David, receive all glory and honor and praises due Him.

Blessed be Jesus, the name above all names, who is our Advocate, the Author and Finisher of our faith, the Consolation of Israel, the Great High Priest, our Messiah, Redeemer, and Emmanuel

Praises be to the Son of Man, the Living Word, the King of Kings and Lord of Lords. May the great I AM who is the Door to heaven and the Vine of eternal life for all who believe continually guide us on our journey to Him. May we accept and receive from the hand of Him who leaves the ninety-nine and searches for the one all things good and holy and wholesome, for He is the only true and Good Shepherd of our souls.

May the Bread of Life sustain His people with words that lead to changed hearts and minds. Let us glory in the Light of the World as He shines into the dark places of our hearts to transform a people acceptable to the only God and Father of us all.

Blessed be the Way and the Truth and the Life, for in Him no one is lost, no falsehood exists, and death has been overcome. Glory be to the Resurrection and the Life, to the One who will call His people to Himself at the trumpet sound and present a bride spotless and pure and holy to Him who is the blessed and righteous and only Potentate of heaven.

May the Cornerstone whom the builders rejected and the Man of Sorrows who was despised and acquainted with grief forever be our bright and shining Morning Star. Praises be to the Prince of Peace, the Lamb of God, the Rose of Sharon, the Elect of God, and the Horn of our Salvation, who is our Faithful Witness.

May the Spirit of the Living God, who is the Breath of the Almighty, be adored and revered and worshipped eternally. Blessed be the Spirit of the Lord God, who is our Spirit of counsel and comfort, knowledge and truth, understanding and wisdom.

We are adopted by the Power of the Highest, who guarantees our inheritance with the Father and breathes into us His Spirit of life and grace and holiness. May the Holy Spirit who embodies the attributes of the one and only Living God empower us with His might to live lives surrendered to the will of the Godhead Three.

Blessings and honor and glory and praises be to the Alpha and Omega, the Beginning and End, the Ancient of Days, the Everlasting Father, Son, and Spirit, who is I AM.

May we go forth to pray for the peoples of the world, secure and confident that as we call upon the names of God, He will provide for us His power, presence, and peace.

Endnotes

1. *The Holy Bible: New International Version* (Grand Rapids: Zondervan, 1984) 1650.

2. *The Holy Bible: New International Version* 1827.

3. *The Holy Bible: New International Version* 1778.

4. *The Holy Bible: New International Version* 1818.

5. *The Holy Bible: New International Version* 1824.

6. *The Holy Bible: New International Version* 1663.

7. *The Holy Bible: New International Version* 1525.

8. *The Holy Bible: New International Version* 1515.

9. *The Passion of the Christ,* dir. Mel Gibson, Icon Productions, 2004.

10. Lorraine Hansberry, *A Raisin in the Sun* (New York: Vintage Books, 1994) 145.

11. *The Holy Bible: New International Version* 1631.

12. *The Holy Bible: New Revised Standard Version* (Nashville: Thomas Nelson, 1989) 91.

13. *The Scarlet and the Black,* dir. Jerry London, ITC and CBS Entertainment Production ,1983.

14. *Wide Awake,* dir. M. Night Shyamalan, Miramax Films, 1998.

15. *The Holy Bible: New International Version* 1820.

16. *The Holy Bible: New International Version* 1529.

17. *The Lord of the Rings: The Fellowship of the Ring,* dir. Peter Jackson, New Line Cinema, 2001.

Sources

Hansberry, Lorraine. *A Raisin in the Sun.* New York: Vintage Books, 1994.

The Holy Bible: New International Version. Grand Rapids: Zondervan, 1984.

The Holy Bible: New Revised Standard Version. Nashville: Thomas Nelson, 1989.

The Passion of the Christ. Dir. Mel Gibson. Perf. James Caviezel, Maia Morgenstern, and Monica Bellucci. Icon Productions, 2004.

The Scarlet and the Black. Dir. Jerry London. Perf. Gregory Peck, Christopher Plummer, and John Gielgud. ITC and CBS Entertainment Production ,1983.

The Lord of the Rings: The Fellowship of the Ring. Dir. Peter Jackson. Perf. Elijah Wood, Sean Astin, Ian McKellen, and Viggo Mortensen. New Line Cinema, 2001.

Wide Awake. Dir. M. Night Shyamalan. Perf. Joseph Cross, Rosie O'Donnell, Dana Delany, and Denis Leary. Miramax Films, 1998.

LaVergne, TN USA
22 April 2010
180089LV00002B/41/P